Copyright © 2023 by Cyril & Dorise Publishing

All rights reserved.

No part of this publication may be reproduced, distributed, or transmitted in any form or by any means, including photocopying, recording, or other electronic or mechanical methods, without the prior written permission of the publisher, except in the case of brief quotations embodied in critical reviews and certain other non-commercial uses permitted by copyright law.

For permission requests, write to the publisher, addressed "Attention:
Permissions Coordinator," at the address below.

Harmony Close,
Kewtown,
Providenciales
Turks & Caicos Islands

ISBN: 9781739369170

https://www.cyrilanddorsiepublishing.com/

THE PROMISE GIFT

TABLE OF CONTENTS

I	Introduction	1
II	True Worship Brings God's Blessing	6
III	The Flesh Must Die	10
IV	Salvation- God's Gift for Mankind	13
V	The Death Walk	15
VI	God's Word Never Changes	19
VII	All The Way	21
VIII	Midnight Has Arrived	23
IX	Don't Allow The Enemy to Stop You	25
X	The Promise Gift	28
XI	Journal	32

Precious Father in heaven, I come before your holy presence right now, asking that you anoint the ears of the readers, especially those reading this book. Open their understanding to the truth of your Word and let those reading realize that you paid the price they couldn't pay; You sent your only-begotten son as a ransom for their sin by dying on the cross as that sacrificial lamb who was slain to wash them clean. You helped them to realize that without the shedding of your blood, there is no remission for sins. Make him or her understand that You truly love them, and by doing this true act of love, you have given them a priceless gift. Help the person reading this book who does not know you to receive you as their personal Lord and Savior. Take them higher so that they carry the gift of promise in Jesus' name.

Amen

CHAPTER 1
Introduction

Chapter One
Introduction

Who is God?
Where does he come from?
Is He real?
If He is real, what must I do to be saved?

Today, many of us are still in the valley of decision making, wondering about questions such as those asked above. Or perhaps you might not be asking any of the above, but I'm sure many are. The one thing that is for sure is we all, at one point in time, will have an appointment with death, whether you are born again, singing in the church choir, serving on the Usher Board, or whatever responsibility or essential role you may play the time will come when you have to do some real soul searching. Let's be honest here: many don't ever attend a church service, but as far as they are concerned, they don't believe true Christians exist, nonetheless acknowledging that there is a God somewhere. It is no surprise that atheists are even in the church; they dance, clap, and sing but have never known what it is to have an authentic experience with the Supreme One. Many of them have a form of godliness but deny its power. Let us continue. The journey will be somewhat lengthy, but it will be worth it.

Many years ago, attending Sunday school, I recalled this question: Who is God?
Many of the Sunday school class gave the same answer: Mary's baby. Yes, of course, we were very young without much knowledge, but as I became older, I began to search the scriptures for myself. To understand God's word, we must be willing to explore the scriptures, for in them are the issues of life. In John 1:1, the scripture tells us that in the beginning was the Word, and the Word was with God, and the Word was God. After reading the scripture, I realized that from the beginning was the Word, and the Word was with God, and the Word was God Himself; everything that God made and created, He spoke into existence.

Genesis 1:3
In the beginning God created the heaven and the earth.
2 And the earth was without form, and void; and darkness was upon the face of the deep. And the Spirit of God moved upon the face of the waters.

3 And God said, Let there be light: and there was light.

We can never taste the goodness of God if we don't believe that he exists. The Word of God tells us in the book of Psalm 14:1, **The fool hath said in his heart, there is no God. They are corrupt, they have done abominable works, there is none that doeth good.**

No one who acts out of the ordinance of God does it with good intentions; they are corrupt, just like the scripture states. We become God's enemy when our hearts are turned toward the world and its wicked systems.

Ye adulterers and adulteresses, know ye not that the friendship of the world is enmity with God? whosoever therefore will be a friend of the world is the enemy of God.

James 4:4

If we are going to be a friend of God, we must be willing and ready to have a genuine relationship with Him. We cannot be true friends of God if we are unwilling to spend quality time knowing who He is and what He has done for us. God is not just a God that you pick up when you like and thrust to the side when you don't want Him. He wants to be a friend to you who sticks closer than a brother or sister; He wants to stay with you in the good and bad times, but for you to have this kind of relationship with Him, you must be willing to study the scriptures and encourage yourself in His word.

John 4:24

God is a Spirit: and they that worship him must worship him in spirit and in truth.

CHAPTER 2

True Worship Brings God's Blessings

Chapter Two
True Worship Brings God's Blessings

Our Lord and Savior want us to be truthful about our worship of Him; to become that worshiper of truth, we must be born again.

Jesus answered and said unto him, Verily, verily, I say unto thee, Except a man be born again, he cannot see the kingdom of God. John 3:3

We must always see and understand the finished work on the cross of Calvary. Our Lord and Savior was willing to take upon Himself our sins, nailed to the cross, He paid a painful price for our sins so that through His shed blood we can be completely free! It was a gift to mankind, but we often fail to become wholly sold out to Him to obtain it.

John 24:1 plainly states that to be a worshiper of God, we must worship in spirit and truth. The Pharisee known as Nicodemus mentioned in John chapter 3 that he came to Jesus by night; he wanted to know the process connected to a man being born again after being conceived from his mother's womb. No doubt, like Nicodemus, many of us may have asked the same question and continue to ask it. However, the answer remains the same: we must be born again. Here, Jesus answered Nicodemus by telling him that except a man is born of "water" and the "spirit," he cannot enter into the kingdom of God. Jesus went on to say to him, that which is born of the flesh is the flesh, and that which is born of the spirit is the spirit. Jesus was straightforward with Nicodemus in many ways: he had to be born again. Similar to Nicodemus, we too have had many questions concerning the second birth, but the truth is to communicate with our Father, we must be able to die to ourselves by killing the flesh so that we can become more spirit-filled.

24 Verily, verily, I say unto you, Except a corn of wheat fall into the ground and die, it abideth alone: but if it die, it bringeth forth much fruit.
25 He that loveth his life shall lose it; and he that hateth his life in this world shall keep it unto life eternal.
John 12:24-25

It is clear from the scriptures that one must die to self in order to inherit the kingdom of God.

For the kingdom of God is not meat and drink; but righteousness, and peace, and joy in the Holy Ghost.
Romans 14:17

So often, we cannot get into God's presence or obtain the peace and tranquillity that we long for because of the many distractions of the flesh and refusing to die to ourselves. If you and I are to take a stand for righteousness and receive the gift of promise, we must be willing to be born again.

Note that Jesus told Nicodemus that he had to be born of the water and the spirit because flesh and blood cannot inherit the kingdom of God.

Now this I say, brethren, that flesh and blood cannot inherit the kingdom of God; neither doth corruption inherit incorruption.
1 Corinthians 15:50

CHAPTER 3

The Flesh Must Die

Chapter Three
The Flesh Must Die

John 12:24-26

24 Verily, verily, I say unto you, Except a corn of wheat fall into the ground and die, it abideth alone: but if it die, it bringeth forth much fruit.
25 He that loveth his life shall lose it; and he that hateth his life in this world shall keep it unto life eternal.
26 If any man serve me, let him follow me; and where I am, there shall also my servant be: if any man serve me, him will my Father honour.

Friends, here, the scripture is evident: to be productive in producing fruit, one must be willing to die to oneself. Taking the death walk indicates that one is ready to be committed to bearing God's fruit, just as our Father was willing to go to the cross to redeem us back to God. We also have our part to play by maintaining that precious gift of salvation and allowing our light to shine so that others may be drawn to him and come to accept His priceless gift that is free of charge. We must first be willing to take this death walk by allowing the guidance of the Holy Spirit to lead us in such a way that we are willing to give up whatever made us prisoners and slaves to sin.

Friends, there is no good thing about the works of the flesh. For you and me to communicate with God, our flesh must first die, as the scripture states. If we are going to keep in the race as good soldiers on the battlefield we need more than just mere salvation, we need to receive all that our Lord and Savior Jesus Christ is giving us, including His resurrection power, dying to ourselves brings the blessings of God. We must be willing to crucify our flesh if we are going to inherit the kingdom of God.

Galatians 5:19-21

**19 Now the works of the flesh are manifest, which are these; Adultery, fornication, uncleanness, lasciviousness,
20 Idolatry, witchcraft, hatred, variance, emulations, wrath, strife, seditions, heresies,
21 Envyings, murders, drunkenness, revellings, and such like: of the which I tell you before, as I have also told you in time past, that they which do such things shall not inherit the kingdom of God.**

CHAPTER 4
Salvation: God's Gift for Mankind

Chapter Four
Salvation-God's Gift for Mankind

For God so loved the world that he gave his only son that whosoever believeth in him shall not perish but have everlasting life.

John 3:16

Growing up as a child, this scripture has been one, if not my favorite, Bible verse. If no one loves me, this scripture verse makes it clear that God does. It is his gift to you and me, and I am more than convinced that if I were the only human being on Earth, He still would have loved me enough to die for me. Think about it, my friends: God is willing to give up His only son to give you and me everlasting life! Yes, friends, God is not selfish. He has proven to you and me how much he loves us, so likewise, we must be willing and ready to go all the way with Him by dying to ourselves. His act of unfailing love must resonate in our hearts if we are to obtain this wonderful gift of promise; we must be willing and ready to go all the way with Him.

22 For as in Adam all die, even so in Christ shall all be made alive.
23 But every man in his own order: Christ the firstfruits; afterward they that are Christ's at his coming.

1 Corinthians 15:22 -23

CHAPTER 5

The Death Walk

Chapter Five
The Death Walk

The scripture made it clear that as all in Adam die, so in Christ, we should be made alive. One can never understand this unless he or she is willing to take the death walk with God in fire baptism. It is evident in scripture that our Lord was not reputable. He was willing to do whatever it took so you and I could obtain the prize; to receive, we must first believe that He is a rewarder to those who diligently seek Him.

And it came to pass, that, while Apollos was at Corinth, Paul having passed through the upper coasts came to Ephesus: and finding certain disciples,

2 He said unto them, Have ye received the Holy Ghost since ye believed? And they said unto him, We have not so much as heard whether there be any Holy Ghost.

3 And he said unto them, Unto what then were ye baptized? And they said, Unto John's baptism.

4 Then said Paul, John verily baptized with the baptism of repentance, saying unto the people, that they should believe on him which should come after him, that is, on Christ Jesus.

5 When they heard this, they were baptized in the name of the Lord Jesus.

6 And when Paul had laid his hands upon them, the Holy Ghost came on them; and they spake with tongues, and prophesied.

Acts 19:1-6

We must never refrain from taking the death walk. Similarly, sometimes you may still wonder about the meaning of the death walk. It simply means dying to oneself and receiving the gift of the Holy Ghost. The scripture states that while passing through the Upper Coast, the Apostle Paul came to Ephesus, where he found certain disciples (they were not unbelievers of the Word of God) whose understanding of the Word of God was not yet activated in its depth, which is similar to many of us today. Please note that the Apostle Paul asked them if they had received the Holy Ghost since they believed.

No wonder many of us are losing the battle; we refuse to become activated by using our spiritual language, which is the gift and evidence that results in speaking in tongues and prophesying. Many tried faking this glorious gift, but this gift can only survive in a temple or body that is living and doing right. Refusal to live and do right will result in demonic influences; many people have a form of godliness but still deny the power of God. The Holy Ghost does the work, not the individual; that is why there are so many so-called worshipers of God who love to be praised. Praise belongs to God; it is God who does the work in us through the power of this beautiful gift, the Holy Ghost. Friends, here the question remains the same: have you received the holy gift since you believed?

Like many of us, our salvation has reached our lips, and so we confess with our mouths and believe in our hearts; however, there's no activation or demonstration of the power of God living inside us. In the same way, you must be willing to go the extra mile to receive the promised gift if you will survive the enemy's fiery darts. Staying in a world without the Holy Ghost is almost impossible! To survive, you must have God's truth living deep inside you.

If we are going to survive in today's world without the Holy Ghost, it will be almost impossible! To survive, we must have the gift of the Holy Ghost living deep within us to pluck up the roots of ancient times planted by the enemy. To become effective, the Word tells us that for the burdens to be lifted from our shoulders and the yoke destroyed, we need a yoke-destroying anointing that is impossible without the Holy Ghost.

And it shall come to pass in that day, that his burden shall be taken away from off thy shoulder, and his yoke from off thy neck, and the yoke shall be destroyed because of the anointing.
Isaiah 10:27

CHAPTER 6

God's Word Never Changes

Chapter Six
God's Word Never Changes

We must be willing and ready to take the next step, just as the disciples did in the Book of Acts. After much explanation concerning John's baptism, they realized that baptism must be done in the name of our Lord Jesus Christ. My friends, there is no doubt that after many years of ups and downs, God's Word remains the same. One can never understand the truth of God's word without searching and reading the scriptures daily. It takes only the Holy Spirit to open our eyes to the truth.

Then opened he their understanding, that they might understand the scriptures,

Luke 24:45

God wants us to become the mighty warriors that He had predestined before time began, but to be effective, we need a fire baptism that will cause hell and all its demons to scramble. Not only will a fire baptism root up and pluck out, but it will be a well springing up inside of you that never goes dry!

I indeed baptize you with water unto repentance. but he that cometh after me is mightier than I, whose shoes I am not worthy to bear: he shall baptize you with the Holy Ghost, and with fire:
Matthew 3:11

CHAPTER 7

All The Way

Chapter Seven
All The Way

When we decide to go all the way with God, He will go all the way with us; accepting the many promises in God's Word is the only way He keeps communicating with us. If we are willing and obedient, we will eat the good of the land, but if we refuse, we will be devoured by the sword. I am sure you are convinced to read on and take the next step that will change your life forever!

19 If ye be willing and obedient, ye shall eat the good of the land:
20 But if ye refuse and rebel, ye shall be devoured with the sword: for the mouth of the Lord hath spoken it.

Isaiah 1:19-20

CHAPTER 8

Midnight Has Arrived

Chapter Eight
Midnight Has Arrived

It is no time to straddle the fence; the late midnight hours are here. We must always be on alert and ready to give all man an answer. We can only do so by putting on our full armor and being fully equipped with the Holy Ghost if we will escape the sword or fiery darts of the evil one.

Many of you can relate that if not for the fire of God, you would have lost many battles, but many likewise cannot, so it is essential to bring clarity to those with blurred visions. If we are to open their eyes to this powerful truth and God's Word, we must be willing to soar like an eagle and have eyes that can see our prey from afar.

Doth the eagle mount up at thy command, and make her nest on high?
Job 39:27

CHAPTER 9

Don't Allow the Enemy to Stop You

Chapter Nine
Don't Allow The Enemy to Stop You

Many today have been beaten up by the evil one, failing to receive the truth of God's word. Can I tell you that you have caused yourself years of unnecessary fights simply because you refuse to accept this gift handed to you as your helper?

And I will pray the Father, and he shall give you another Comforter, that he may abide with you for ever;

17 Even the Spirit of truth; whom the world cannot receive, because it seeth him not, neither knoweth him: but ye know him; for he dwelleth with you, and shall be in you.

John 14:16-17

My friend, it is clear that no one who is God's enemy can receive this powerful gift, the spirit of truth because God does not dwell in unclean temples. I have had multiple experiences with false teachers and prophets who claimed to be teaching and prophesying. Still, under a false flow, true anointing always brings God's blessings, and where the power of God is, yokes are destroyed, and burdens are always lifted. God has not called us to become bound by religion, nor does He make slaves of His people.

His plan for mankind is that they live in His divine peace and presence. Salvation is handed down to man as a gift; we don't have to pay for it, yet we have been beaten up to pay the church rent, buy some pastors Gucci shoes, and Mercedes-Benz.

Friends, let's be honest: if the Holy Ghost is free and lives deep within us, we must have good discernment of the things that bring God glory and those that do not. It is time we wake up and be the church He calls us to be! When our eyes are not open to this spiritual truth, we will become wrecked, frustrated, and useless to ourselves and God. I am addressing this because, for many years, the church has been persecuted. After all, we refused to know our rights. If you are attending a ministry that refuses to teach and preach about the real power of God and has failed to pursue after holiness, it is high time to make that decision to get out.

John 14:26

But the Comforter, which is the Holy Ghost, whom the Father will send in my name, he shall teach you all things, and bring all things to your remembrance, whatsoever I have said unto you.

CHAPTER 10

The Promise Gift

Chapter Ten
The Promise Gift

Ephesians 2:8-9

**8 For by grace are ye saved through faith; and that not of yourselves: it is the gift of God:
9 Not of works, lest any man should boast.**

The Holy Spirit wants to become your friend living deep inside of you; He wants to be that still, small voice that directs your pathway, but to have Him living deep down inside, you must be willing and ready to accept Him as your personal Savior and friend.

Many today are feeling a void that they cannot explain. If you are like them, why not invite Him into your heart right now? Don't you think He is speaking? Will you let Him in? He is that priceless gift you and I cannot afford. Yes, my friends, it is the only gift that can fulfill the emptiness we feel inside; He is the only one that can fulfill that longing. Letting Him be a part of our life is the best decision you and I could ever make. All God wants is a yes to His will and His way.

Jeremiah 29:11

For I know the thoughts that I think toward you, saith the Lord, thoughts of peace, and not of evil, to give you an expected end.

Friends, the Holy Ghost will be your software and computer. You will need no better system to process the required information and no better source to remind you when data is low. Data will only go low if you haven't charged your spiritual battery! God has given us everything we will ever need through the working of His Holy Spirit. What an incredible gift to you and me. We must awaken out of this deep, dark sleep and exercise our spiritual authority by demonstrating this awesome gift of promise to the world!

For the promise is unto you, and to your children, and to all that are afar off, even as many as the Lord our God shall call.
Acts 2:39

ABOUT
THE AUTHOR

Apostle Rosemary Duncanson is a unique and rare vessel to the body of Christ. Apostle Duncanson was born in the Turks and Caicos Islands; she is a mother, Pastor, and Teacher. Having proclaimed the Word of God for more than three decades, her yoke-breaking anointing has helped many across all spheres of life. Apostle Dunacanson enjoys her outreach ministries and reaches out to as many as possible, calling darkness into light. After many years of pain, hurt, and disappointments, she is proving her ministries entirely and is determined that the enemy will not win. Her determination has given her recognition in every area of her life.

Letters To God

Letters To God

Letters To God

Letters To God

Letters To God

Letters To God

Letters To God

Letters To God

Letters To God

Letters To God

Letters To God

www.ingramcontent.com/pod-product-compliance
Lightning Source LLC
Chambersburg PA
CBHW061147170426
43209CB00011B/1586